Old Norwich

Michael Chandler

The Regent Theatre opened in 1923 with the production *Dorothy* which had a cast of over 70. Although the local papers called it a 'lavish production', it was not a financial success and an overdraft of £130 was required from Barclays Bank, which was guaranteed by the Lord Mayor, Lady Manse, surgeon Sir Hamilton Balance and Ivan Spain. The play showing in this 1934 photo is *Wonder Bar*, based on the film staring Al Jolson. Today the building is a night club.

Stenlake Publishing Ltd, 2013

text © Michael Chandler, 2013
Photographs © George A F Plunkett
First Published in the United Kingdom, 2013
Stenlake Publishing Limited
54-58 Mill Square, Catrine, KA5 6RD
www.stenlake.co.uk

ISBN 978-1-84033-613-9

Dedicated to Ross and to the good citizens of Norwich who care for its heritage.

FOREWORD

Few cities can boast of a heritage as rich as Norwich's. Visitors wonder at the churches which have dominated the city's skyline for centuries, and the beautiful architecture which sits on Europe's largest intact medieval street pattern. Formerly England's second city, the city of Norwich benefits today from its prosperous past as a home of considerable mercantile wealth and cultural activity.

The face of Norwich has changed considerably in recent decades – admittedly not all of them for the better. Three Baedeker Raids during the Second World War, targeted at Norwich because of its heritage value, destroyed hundreds of buildings including Bonds of Norwich department store. Further deliberate damage has been caused by poor planning decisions – such as the demolition of the Norwich Hippodrome to make way for St. Giles multi-storey car park. Despite this, Norwich remains one of the most attractive cities in the UK.

George Plunkett has left Norwich a permanent legacy in the form of thousands of images which have captured the city's development from the 1930s to the new millennium. Michael Chandler has a real passion for Norwich and its history. His depth of knowledge and eagerness to share the stories of the city and its people is apparent to anyone who has met him.

For better and for worse, social, political and economic drivers during the 20th century are behind the Norwich that we know and love today. I hope you will, like me, find this book to be a fascinating insight into the city's past and present.

Simon Wright
Member of Parliament for Norwich South

ABOUT THE AUTHOR

Michael Chandler was born in London in 1962. He has been involved in the media business most of his working life and first came to Norwich in 1992 for a long weekend break. In 2006 he made the move to Norwich and quickly found the city a fascinating subject to research. Soon he was involved in making a documentary about the Medieval house under the Magistrates Court for ITV Anglia History Channel. He then began giving talks about Norwich and its history to local history groups and in 2010 his first book *Murder & Crime Norwich* was published by The History Press. Michael has appeared on BBC Look East, BBC Radio Norfolk and Radio Norwich.

ACKNOWLEDGEMENTS

Brent Johnson, British Journal of Nursing, Christina Cole, *Eastern Daily Press*, Gallyon & Sons, Gordon Rooney, Jack Walters, James E Broughton, Joe Mason (www.joemasonpage.wordpress.com), *London Gazette*, Michael Crouch, National Grid Archives, Norfolk County Council, Norfolk Heritage Centre, Norfolk Record Office, www.norfolkpubs.co.uk, www.racns.co.uk, Simon Wright MP for Norwich South, the Marks & Spencer Archive and the continued support from Richard Stenlake and all at Stenlake Publishing. I would also like to thank the many people who contacted me with their amazing stories of Old Norwich.

ABOUT THE PHOTOGRAPHER

George Plunkett on St. James' Hill 1931

George Arthur Frank Plunkett was born in 1913 at home in Dereham Road. He served with the Royal Air Force from January 1941 until February 1946.

George acquired a 'box' camera in 1931 and started building a photographic survey of Norwich. Aware of its limitations, he replaced the box camera the following year with an Ensign Carbine number 7 which lasted the rest of his life. He developed and printed over 1,000 rolls of black and white film himself, arranging the contact-sized prints in albums according to subject matter or street name. From 1938 to 1952 he was a member of the Norwich and District Photographic Society. From 1935 until his death he was also a member of the Norfolk and Norwich Archaeological Society. He had five papers published in the Society's Transactions: *Old Norwich Doorways* (1942); *17th Century Ceiling at 12 St Stephen's Street, Norwich* (1944); *St George (Middle) Street, Norwich – In Memoriam* (1970); *Churchman House, St Giles' Street, Norwich* (1975); and *Norfolk Church Screens (1865 Survey)* (1979). All except the last-named were illustrated with his own photographs. The paper on Norfolk screens resulted from his transcribing the 320 replies which had been received in response to a questionnaire sent out by the Archaeological Society in 1865 to the Norfolk clergy. He also was a member of the Royal Archaeological Institute from 1951 to 1970, publishing a paper entitled *Norwich Guildhall*.

Self portrait in mirror, 1933.

In March 1973 he retired from local government having reached the age of 60. In September 1987 he had a book *Disappearing Norwich* published by Daltons of Lavenham. It was illustrated by 120 of his photographs, mainly from the 1930s, when slum clearance and street-widening were responsible for the demolition of many buildings of architectural or historical importance. Sales of the book were sufficiently good to justify two reprints. In November 1990 Daltons published his *Rambles in Old Norwich*. Illustrated with 148 of his photographs, it was in the nature of a perambulation not only of the four Great Wards of the city but also of the area outside the walls. Unlike the previous book where all the illustrations were of things no longer existing, in this book a number of views were included

George with sons Philip and John at Clifton Zoo, 1962

of buildings still standing although with a history perhaps not all that well known.

In 2000, all his photographs of the city were placed on the Internet at the website www.georgeplunkett.co.uk. The website has generated a steady stream of emails from appreciative visitors from around the world. George had enjoyed an active and independent life until, at the age of 93 in 2006, he was brought down by a combination of pneumonia and a small stroke following a fall.

George and Margaret Plunkett 1986

INTRODUCTION

The Kingdom of East Angles was founded by bringing together North and South Folk in the year 520. Originally called Fybriggate, Magdalen Street was the main street of the Anglo Saxon town. Before the arrival of William I and the Norman Conquest, the people of Norwich paid Edward the Confessor an annual tax of £20, six jars of honey, one bear, and six baiting dogs.

In 1194 Norwich was granted the status of a city under Richard I but was excluded from any jurisdiction over the castle, which belonged to the king, and any jurisdiction over the cathedral priory, which belonged to the bishop. City walls with twelve gates were built between 1297 and 1334. To save on repairs, the city gates were demolished between 1791-1808.

During the reign of Queen Elizabeth I, Norwich Priest Matthew Parker was made Archbishop of Canterbury. A man of intention to every detail he earned the nickname 'Nosey Parker'. The first provincial newspaper in England the *Norwich Post* was printed by Francis Burges in 1701. Reformer Elizabeth Fry who appears on the back of the five pound note (until 2016) was born in Magdalen Street in 1780. In 1792, wine merchant and Kent banker Thomas Bignold set up Norwich Union (now AVIVA).

By 1801 the population of Norwich was in the region of 36,000 and it was one of the largest cities in Britain, although it was soon to be taken over by others. Parts of the city became overcrowded and there were several outbreaks of typhoid, cholera, diphtheria and smallpox.

Jeremiah Colman moved from Bawburgh to Stoke Holly Cross in 1804 and produced mustard. His nephew Jeremiah James Colman moved the business to Carrow to be near to the city in 1856. Jarrolds came to Norwich in 1823 and started a print shop in London Street and by 1836 Norwich had its first police force. *Norfolk News* was started by the families of the Colmans, Copemans and Tilletts in 1844 and went on to become the *Eastern Daily Press* and *Eastern Evening News*. From 1849 there was a train service to London.

In 1857 the first public library was opened. Clearance of slums started in 1877. The Royal Arcade was built in 1899 by George Skipper and by the following year trams were running in Norwich and serving a population of 100,000 people. The trams ran until 1933 when they were bought over and replaced by buses. In 1938 City Hall was completed. During the Second World War over 3,000 houses were damaged in air raids.

The Castle Mall Shopping Centre opened in 1993 at a cost of £145 million pounds but the focus of the book is "Old Norwich" - a combination of the historical (the genuinely old) and the disappeared/lost (quite often the former).

Hardwick House was built by the London-based architect, Philip Charles Hardwick, for the Harvey and Hudson Bank. This became known as the Crown Bank, having taken on the business of Norwich Bank which had closed in 1808 with debts of over £460,000. Under director Sir Robert Harvey, the Crown Bank itself failed and Sir Robert took his own life. At the time there were over thirty branches in Norfolk, Suffolk and Cambridgeshire. The remaining directors of the bank filed for bankruptcy and most of the premises were sold to Gurney & Co. Investors got back 10s. 6d. in the pound.

By 1875 Hardwick House had become Norwich's general post office and was still this in 1938 at the time of the photograph. The original post office had been situated in Post Office Street, near to Market Place and received two deliveries from London daily. In 1969 the post office moved to a building in Bank Plain and in 1971 Hardwick House was sold to a property company in London and then became part of Anglia Television.

The Carlton was opened in 1932 by Mr. V. E. Harrison (who already owned many cinemas in the Norwich area) but was later taken over by the Odeon Group. The Hallé Orchestra, founded in Manchester by Sir Charles Hallé, performed there. The building went on to be known as the Gaumont before closing and becoming a bingo hall. This atmospheric night photograph with the building all lit up dates from 1935.

Robert Herne Bond was born in Ludham. In 1879 he and his wife Mary purchased a small drapery shop at 19 Ber Street. By 1895 he had purchased several properties alongside, and also nos. 62 and 64 Bridge Street. By the start of the 1900s Bond's had become the largest millinery outlet outside London's West End. Bond died in 1924 and his son William took over the business, soon joined by his brother Ernest. By 1939 Bond's employed over 200 people, and it claimed that on one day's trading it served 13,000 customers. Early in the morning on Saturday 27th June 1942, during a Baedeker raid in the area, 16 people were killed and 117 private houses and 30 shops and offices were destroyed, including Bond's. Within three days of the bombing, Ernest had started trading again after purchasing a fleet of buses that were parked in the car park and filled them with stock. Staff at Bond's had to serve a three year apprenticeship and all worked on commission. Apprentices received a Christmas box gift of ten shillings. After the war, Bond's was rebuilt as shown in this 1955 picture and the new policy was to move from selling cheap products and to go upmarket, which proved to be a good decision.

Next door to the Capitol was the Lido Ballroom. Both buildings were later transformed into the Norwood Rooms. George White's *Scandals* were being shown in 1934. These were Broadway revues based on the Ziegfeld Follies and featuring the George White Girls. The films included stars of the day such as Alice Faye, Eleanor Powell, Rudy Vallee and The Three Stooges.

Once known as Motstowe, Bank Plain housed Gurney's Bank. The English author Ralph Hale Mottram, was the son of the chief clerk of the bank and grew up in Bank House. The family were nonconformists and worshipped at the Octagon Chapel, Colegate. Ralph was mayor in 1953 and a great defender of Mousehold Heath, stating that it was the property of all those born in Norwich. When he was four years old he chose Rosary Cemetery as his final resting place. The photo dates from 1936.

A row of 19th century houses used to be along the side of this road which is now the Inner Link road. 4 to 8 Barn Road were terraced three storey houses, whose frontages were constructed with knapped flints. The rear walls backed on to St. Benedict's Back Lane. The houses, seen here in 1938, were built between 1779 and 1789 and were redeveloped in the 19th century. During the evening of 27th April 1942 a bomb fell on the area causing severe damage to the houses. The Omnibus Public House, which by the 1900s was also known as Harcourts was destroyed by enemy action.

Barrack Street, on the east side of the city, has also been known as St. James Street, Pockthorpe Street, Barregate and Bargate Street and was the site of the cavalry barracks, built on the site of an old manor house in 1791 for £20,000. At one time it housed 320 men and 266 horses. A high wall surrounded the whole of the barracks site which was about ten acres in total. Opposite the barracks, on a piece of land known as the Hospital Meadow, was the Dungeon Tower, which was a large brick building, originally surrounded by a battlement which had been built as a prison for the cathedral precincts. The area was mainly home to weavers and spinners. In 1933 Barrack Street became a clearance area as the tiny houses were crammed together, sharing outside toilets and wash houses. The whole area was so infested with rats that they did not bother to run away if approached in broad daylight.

By the early 1900s there were twelve public houses on Barrack Street. The Pockthorpe Brewery of Steward and Patteson at one stage was sending out over 100,000 barrels of beer a year. The brewery site covered about twelve acres. In 1793 John Patteson had purchased a brewery that was owned by Charles Greeves. After he retired in 1820, his son, John Stainforth Patteson took over along with Donald Steward, and traded under the name of Steward, Patteson & Steward. In 1832 Henry Staniforth Patteson joined the firm. After purchasing Finch's Brewery in 1837 the company became known as Steward, Patteson, Finch & Co. before settling on the name Steward & Patteson.

Situated at No. 1 Ber Street was in 1936 Thomas Hastings the greengrocers, listed in *Kelly's Directory* as being a potato and banana merchant with another shop at No. 2 All Saints Street. Next door at Nos. 3, 5, 7 and 11 was Patrick's Stores, outfitters, footwear and clothing specialists. Behind can just be seen the building of Mann, Arthur. N, pawnbroker of 1 and 3 All Saints Green. In 1942 the building was hit by air raids and a few months later the greengrocers was demolished.

Opposite Bonds at 16 Ber Street and also destroyed during enemy action in June 1942 was the premises of G. J. Woods & Sons, a chair basket and sieve works company shown here as it was when photographed in 1936. In a publication published in 1940, the company claimed that it was the only company in England to make sedge horse collars.

Bonds sold the 70 feet site for Agricultural House, the offices of the National Farmers' Union, at 23 Ber Street, for £1,750. In April 1951 R G Carter's tender to erect the building was accepted and it opened in July 1952, a few years before this photo was taken. Members met there for 46 years, with executive meetings being held on Saturdays.

The mural on the side of the Ber Street Gates public house at 174 Ber Street in this 1938 photo shows the gate with portcullis flanked by one tower. Commissioned by Morgan's Brewery, it was originally drawn by John Kirkpatrick and was reproduced in engravings by Henry Ninham. John Moray Smith added some vegetation, people and flags in 1937.

Bethel Street in 1962 with the library building approaching completion. It occupied space between Bethel Street and Theatre Street on what had previously been Lady's Lane, which was then renamed Esperanto Way. Esperanto was a universal language created by Polish doctor Ludovic Zamenhof in an utopian vision that he thought would bring people together by means of a shared language, but the idea never fully took off although it still has its followers.

In 1934 the Mancroft Restaurant in Bethel Street was owned by Mrs. Jesse Sneath, who in 1919 was also the landlady of the Mancroft Stores, which in 1911 were known as The Eldon Stores.

Between Nos. 20 and 36 Bethel Street were Blazeby's Yard and Jay's Court which were demolished during slum clearance to make way for the new fire station. In this 1933 photograph the buildings have been partially demolished. Holes were found housing civil war period ammunition. In the same block was the Coach Makers Arms. Landlord Peter Rout was convicted in 1890 of failing to admit the police and was fined £2 plus 17s. 6d. in costs and in 1900 landlady Susannah Elizabeth Rout was fined £2 plus 7s. costs or 14 days detention for permitting drunkenness.

Top left: This house at 53 Bethel Street was built in the second half of the Georgian period and was the home of many well-known (at the time) dignitaries, including Dr. Edward Copeman who worked at the Norfolk and Norwich Hospital from 1851 to 1878. He was a gifted musician and played at many of the Norwich festivals. Surgeon Mr. F. C. Bailey also lived here as did as Dr. G. S. B. Long. By the 1940s the house was owned and run by the Diocesan Refuge.

Top right: Between Nos. 55 and 57 Bethel Street, shown here in 1936, was Watts' Court which was bombed during the evening of 27th June 1942. Watts' Court took its name from the merchant John Langley Watts who was sheriff in 1771 and mayor in 1774.

Lower left: Bethel Street was once called Upper Newport. The town crier Nathaniel Easthaugh lived at No. 43. Knipe Gobbret who was mayor in 1771 lived there, as did Frederick William Harmer, owner of the clothing company F. W. Harmer & Co., who had their factory here. F. W. Harmer & Co was the oldest firm of clothing manufacturers in the country. William Harmer joined the firm in 1850 and stayed there for 50 years. In 1880 he was elected an alderman of the city and four years later he was appointed justice of the peace. Mayor between 1887-88, he was also one of the founders of the Norwich Electricity Co., Ltd. The Harmer family had been involved with manufacturing since 1701. The Mancroft works in Bethel Street eventually became too cramped for the company and in 1890 a large factory and warehouse was built in St. Andrew's Street.

9-15 Bishopgate in 1936. Near to here, Lord Edmund Sheffield was killed during Kett's Rebellion of 1549. For many years there was a letter 'S' in the pavement that marked the spot. By the middle of the 19th century the stone had been moved to the corner, but by the 1860s it has been moved to the present spot and built into the wall at the expense of Dr. Charles Williams, who also placed another stone with the letter 'S' on the ground to show the location. However, this was later covered up with asphalt.

During the 19th century this area was known as Tabernacle Street. Just by the Adam and Eve public house was the Tabernacle, a 1,000 seater church which opened in 1755. It's shown here in 1936. The architect was Thomas Ivory, who also designed St. Helens and the Theatre Royal. The Methodist Rev. James Wheatley, a cobbler from Wales, preached there. Up to 2,000 people would listen to him preach but a group of men from the Hell Fire Club at the Bell Hotel took delight in attacking him, which resulted in rioting, until the Dragoons were called in to restore order. Two years after the Tabernacle opened, Rev. James Wheatley left Norwich in disgrace after being accused of improper conduct with a female member of the congregation.

A view of the gas works in 1965. The British Gas Light Company's head office was situated on the corner of Dereham Road and Heigham Street. On the right of the photo is The Adam and Eve, one of Norwich's oldest public houses which claims to be haunted by the ghost of Lord Sheffield who was killed nearby during Kett's Rebellion.

The Great Hospital was founded in 1249 by Bishop Walter de Suffield to care for aged priests, scholars and paupers. It is the only surviving medieval hospital whose documents survive intact. The plaque in the picture above the door reads as follows:

> King Henry the Eight of noble fame bequeath'd this city, this commodious place with lands and rents, he did endow the same to help decreped age in woful case. Edward the Sixth that Prince of Royal stem perform'd his fathers generous bequest. Good Queen Elizabeth imitating them. Ample endowments added to the rest. Their pious deeds we gratefully record. While heaven them crowns with glorious reward.

Top right: Botolph Street takes its name from the former Church of St. Buttolph the Abbot. Botolph Street leading up to Stump Cross was closed in 1969, three years after this photograph was taken and then demolished to make way for the Anglia Square shopping development.

Bottom right: Chamberlin's factory, 1967. Built in 1903 by the architect A. F. Scott (who went on to design the building for Buntings the drapers on the corner of Rampant Horse Street and St. Stephens) this was originally the clothing factory for Chamberlins. In 1949 it was occupied by Roberts the Printers, which was one of the many businesses to suffer when the street was demolished to make way for Anglia Square.

Below: The business of P. Segger (Norwich) Ltd, boot and shoe manufacturer traded from No. 53 Botolph Street for many years before going into liquidation in July 1972. This view of the premises dates from 1936.

Below: 1 Calvert Street, shown here in 1936, dates back to the early 18th century. It has been restored on numerous occasions and has now been converted into flats. Calvert Street may have been named after John Calvert who was sheriff in 1741. Robert Partridge, mayor in 1784, resided at No. 1 and Herbert Frazer who was lord mayor in 1936-37 was born here.

Above: Between the two world wars, this building on the west side of Calvert Street at Nos. 3-5 was a shoe factory, and like most of the buildings in the area it had fallen into disrepair as evidenced by this 1936 photo. It was destroyed by enemy action on 2nd August 1942, and the properties opposite were badly damaged.

The Methodist chapel and manse, captured in this 1936 picture, was built in 1810. It closed on Sunday 26th June 1966 to make way for the inner link road.

The Castle Hotel lit up at night for the Silver Jubilee in 1935. The hotel typically boasted in its advertising that *No matter what the occasion, the "Castle" can rise to it. Without fuss. Without a frown – and – without frightening you with an enormous bill afterwards. That's because the "Castle" is a professional hotel … run by professionals who enjoy their jobs, and, above all, it's a friendly hotel, which is probably why the "Castle" is the centre of so much of East Anglia's social activity these days. Next time you feel like an evening out, or an all out we've-got-something-to-celebrate-good-time, make it the "Castle" - you'll be glad you did.*

Demolition work at the Castle Hotel starting in 1990. Originally called the Castle Inn in 1664 and then the Castle Hotel from 1665, its address was given as 14 White Lion Street in 1783 and 13 White Lion Street in 1802. It was accidentally damaged by a fire in 1940.

Caley's chocolate factory, 2003. Albert Jarman Caley came to Norwich in 1857 and established a chemist shop in London Street. By 1863 he was making mineral waters including soda, potash, seltzer, lemonade and ginger ale, and was soon joined in the business by his son Edward and then his brothers Frederick and Stuart. In 1883 the firm started to make cocoa, and then in 1886 chocolate. The company took over a factory in Chapelfield known as the Fleur de Lys. In 1887 the motive power that Caleys required was 18 h.p. It soon was raised to 260 h.p. By 1904 the company was employing 700 people and their chocolate and Christmas crackers were being shipped all over the world. In London they traded from Bond Street and had a depot in Hanover Square. The company used a Swiss type plant to produce the chocolate and the milk came from Garrett Taylor's celebrated herd of red poll cattle at Whitlingham. Their chocolate bars were popular with soldiers during the First World War, with their most famous brand being 'Marching Chocolate.'

The company took an interest in the moral and social welfare of all its staff, and employed a permanent lady visitor who conducted classes for the girls and visited any of those who were ill. A cricket club was set up for the men. The Caley family kept the business until 1918 when it was sold to The African and Eastern Trade Corporation, who in turn sold out to John Mackintosh & Sons Limited. This company later merged with Rowntree which itself was taken over by Nestle in 1988. The factory closed for business on 29th November 1996.

Left: The Lord Camden public house was situated in the Lord Camden Yard by 15-17 Charing Cross and was in business from around 1806 until the 1920s. The yard itself was demolished during the widening of Charing Cross in the 1920s. The picture dates from 1939, after its demolition.

Right: On the opposite side of the road at 64-74 Colegate Jewson & Sons Limited had their head office, seen here in 1936. The business was started in Huntingdonshire in 1840 by George Jewson and transferred to Norwich in 1868.

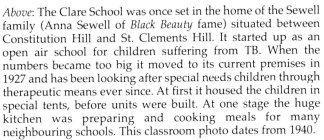

Above: The Clare School was once set in the home of the Sewell family (Anna Sewell of *Black Beauty* fame) situated between Constitution Hill and St. Clements Hill. It started up as an open air school for children suffering from TB. When the numbers became too big it moved to its current premises in 1927 and has been looking after special needs children through therapeutic means ever since. At first it housed the children in special tents, before units were built. At one stage the huge kitchen was preparing and cooking meals for many neighbouring schools. This classroom photo dates from 1940.

Right: Opposite St. James Church Graveyard at 106 Cowgate a timber-framed house, called Fastolf's House, which was numbered 104-108 stood out. In its early days it had 14 bedrooms and there were three smaller buildings in the yard at the rear of the house. By 1830 it had become a pub trading under the name The Ship Inn, which it remained until 1904, when it became occupied by many families. In July 1938, three years after this photo was taken, it was purchased by the city corporation for £470. This once great historical 15th century house then stood empty until 1948 when, along with other homes it was demolished. Sir John Fastolf, the original owner, had many properties in England and France, including Blickling Hall. Born in 1378 at Caistor Manor House, he made his name in the French Wars and participated in the Battle of Agincourt in 1418. He moved to Norfolk and spent the last few years of his life there before dying in 1459 and being buried at St. Benet's Abbey.

The original golden eagle and pearl was put up by silversmith Isaac March in 1769. The sign in the picture is a replica, created by John Culyer in 1869. Bonser's took over the business around 1875 and purveyed groceries, provisions, wines and spirits from these premises at 10 Davey Place. The owners were J. Utting in partnership with William Plunkett, the great uncle of George Plunkett. The business was later owned by E. C. Sennitt, who also had shops in St. Stephen's and Goat Lane. The golden eagle and pearl sign was eventually presented to Norwich Castle Museum.

At the end of the street the sign for The King's Head can be seen in this 1961 streetscape. The original public house was pulled down when Davey Place was created in 1813. It was called The Henry VIII well into the 20th century. John Davey, landlord 1845-46, was probably the cousin to Alderman Jonathan Davey, whom coincidentally this pedestrian way is named after. Landlord James Fenn was convicted in 1871 of being open out of hours. In 1945 Alfred George Craft was accused on two cases of suffering gaming, and he received an absolute discharge, meaning that although found guilty he received no punishment.

At the time they closed down for business in 1959 Harry Tyce and Son of Davey Place were known as the oldest ironmongers in the city. The firm was founded by John Browne, who was mayor in 1788. It first opened in 1750 in St. Peter's Street and was later sold to Edward Orams, who was sheriff in 1889 and who went into partnership with Harry Tyce. When Tyce's son retired the business ended. The photo shows the frontage in the year of closure still as it had been in the 19th century.

Nos. 5 to 7 Dereham Road was where the new cinema was to be built when this photo was taken in 1937. Note St. Benedicts Garage next door but one, which is still standing after the redevelopment has taken place (see next picture).

The Regal was built by Thomas Gill & Son, a Norwich based building firm to designs by architects J. Owen Bond and Son of Tombland and had a thousand seats and a cafe for the patrons. It opened on 17th April 1938 showing the film *Rose Marie* starring Nelson Eddy and Jeannette MacDonald. This cinema, operated by independent exhibitor Victor E. Harrison, closed down in the 1960s and became the Mayfair Bingo Club.

The electricity works floodlit at night, 1937. Francis Maddison Long was born in 1867 and died in June 1939. Educated at Westminster School and also by private tuition, he went on to study electrical engineering at King's College, London, and then from 1887 to 1889 was articled as a pupil to Professor H. Robinson, consulting engineer, of Westminster Council who then later employed by him as an assistant engineer on the preparation of plans for civil engineering works and for the St. Pancras electric lighting scheme. In 1892 he became resident engineer of the Norwich Electricity Co. in connection with the erection of the Duke Street works and the laying of mains. When this was completed he was appointed engineer and manager to the company, and when in 1903 the Corporation took over the undertaking he became the city electrical engineer. He retired in 1932, but later became a director of the West Morland and District Electricity Supply Co. While at Norwich he took particular interest in the development of electrical supply in rural areas. He also devised the two-part tariff in which there is a fixed charge based on the assessment and a low charge per unit consumed.

The Duke of Norfolk's palace stood here at what is now St. Andrews car park. The palace was rebuilt in 1602 and again in 1672 and was demolished in 1711 due to a disagreement between the duke and Mayor Thomas Havers. The domestic offices were turned into a workhouse, and later it became the Duke's Palace Public House which stood there until the late 1960s when a multi-storey car park was built.

This building, the Red Lion public house, was built by Robert Holmes, who became sheriff in 1646. Above the door is his initials 'R.F.H' and the year 1643. It is one of the finest examples of a house from that date in Norwich, and in 1954 it was accorded Grade II Listed status. A building has been on this site since 1582. In the early 1900s commuters were provided with a stable so they could leave their horses and take a tram into the city. It is still a pub.

The Reverend Joseph Leycester Lyne, better known as Father Ignatius will always be remembered for trying to restore monastic life to the Church of England. Gladstone regarded him as one of the greatest orators of his life, whilst the well-known atheist, Bradlaugh stated that Ignatius was a man whose influence he most feared. By 1869 he had acquired part of the mountainside above Capel-y-ffin, a hamlet near the English-Welsh border in Powys, and built a monastery. Ignatius later set up a community at Norwich known as the Priory of St. Mary and St. Dunstan. He raised funds to establish a church, but this was unsuccessful. Ignatius went on a pilgrimage to Rome in 1866 and after this returned to Norwich. An aggressive man, he was well-known for threatening those who opposed him with eternal damnation, and three people who took issue with him died within 24 hours. Although buried in the chancel floor of the Abbey Church in Capel-y-ffin under a tiled cross his spirit is said to appear in Elm Hill with a bible in his hand cursing passers-by.

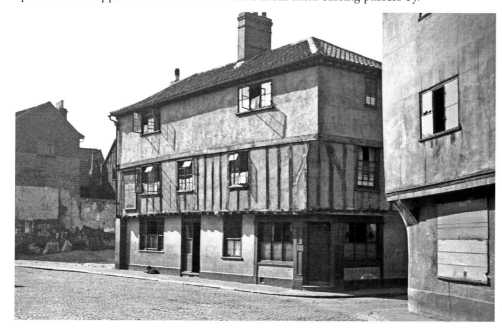

The Tiger stood on the corner of Fishergate. Seen here in 1939, it was also known during its time as the Wounded Tiger and the Tiger Tavern.

Anguish's school in Fishergate was named after its founder Thomas Anguish, who was mayor in 1611. Also sometimes referred to as the Bluecoat or Bluebottle school on account of the colour of the uniforms, the school opened on 1st January 1621 and twelve children attended initially. In 1664 the girls were sent to a separate school in nearby Golden Dog Lane as a result of a bequest of Robert Baron, who was mayor in 1649. By the 18th century there were up to 36 children all attired in blue coats and red hats. The school closed in 1885 and finances were put aside from a fund set up by Anguish to help boys into secondary school and apprenticeships. Today Anguish's Education Foundation has its offices at St. Benedict Street.

The tram is on East Side on first traffic day in 1933 en route to Unthank Road and Magdalen Street. The Norwich Electric Tramways Company was owned by the New General Traction Company. Work on building the tramway commenced in June 1898 and it started operating in July 1900. In the background is F. J. Bugg Ltd., Boot and Leather Factors. In better days the company had owned the third motor car ever to be registered in Norwich (license plate AH3) but in August 1939 it went into voluntary liquidation.

Photographed in 1937 this 15th century stone shaft is in Fyebridge Street situated between Wensum Street and Magdalen Street. The house was built for Edmund Wood, a grocer and sheriff in 1536, then mayor in 1548. His son Robert also became mayor and was knighted by Elizabeth I when she visited Norwich. The original house remains behind its 18th century frontage and was cemented over after it was exposed (and the photograph taken) in 1987. The spandrels of its doorway now form part of the doorway at 24 Princes Street.

In 1938 the road was extended between Gaol Hill and Gentlemen's Walk. The war memorial, which was erected in 1927, can be seen in front of the Guildhall. Chamberlins department store is behind and next to it is Spalls, fancy good dealers who sold brooches, necklaces and ornaments and Dean & Palmer, tailors where a new suit would cost £12 10s. in 1949 when most working men had a wage of around £5 per week.

Grove Road's Surrey Inn traded as the Ram Inn until 1845. Damaged during enemy air raids between 27th and 29th April 1942 it operated from a shed until it was fully repaired and continued in business until closing in 1955 after a compulsory purchase was announced. In this 1939 photograph a horse-drawn milk float has stopped outside. The milkman would wear a uniform including a white cap and apron and the milk was sold in glass bottles. During the Second World War a family was allowed three pints of milk a week, sometimes only two.

The Haymarket Picture House opened in 1911 to the designs of architect J. Owen Bond. It was a conversion of a former London & Provincial Bank building and had additions made in 1921 as a result of which it had an increased seating capacity of 1,687 with a restaurant attached. It reopened in February 1929 showing the film *The Singing Fool* starring Al Jolson. In June 1930 it was taken over by Denman Picture Houses Ltd. In 1954 it was renamed the Gaumont, but it closed down in August of that year and was demolished to make way for shops.

In 1959 when this photo was taken Walt Disney's *Darby O'Gill and the Little People*, starring Albert Sharpe, Janet Munro, Sean Connery and Jimmy O'Dea was showing at the Gaumont. When it closed the Gaumont name transferred to the Carlton.

This photograph of Peter Robinson's store was taken in 1962, the shop situated where the Haymarket and Gaumont cinemas used to be. Today the store is Top Shop and Top Man.

On the left of the picture is the St. George and the Dragon public house, which traded from 1763 to 1988. It's seen here in 1932. The pub was originally named George and Dragon in the 19th century, then just the George in the 1930s, then back to George and Dragon in the 1950s and when it closed in 1988 it was Saint George and Dragon. Renovations in the 1970s uncovered ancient timber beams, which were replaced by polystyrene replicas. In 1990 it was occupied by a building society and in 2002 became a McDonalds.

Francis Lambert came from an old Roman Catholic family and was the first tea dealer in Norwich to appreciate the merits of Indian teas and how to use them in the blends he sold. His son Francis Jerome joined the business in 1874. The first branch to open was at Broad Row, Great Yarmouth, and this was followed by shops in St. Stephen's Street and then Magdalen Street. In London Street the letters 'L.O.C.' puzzled many people until it was shown to mean 'Lambert's Oriental Café.' Customers collected wrappers from BOP (Broken Orange Pekoe tea) and could redeem them in exchange for a packet of tea. Next is here now.

The statue of Sir. Thomas Browne by Henry Albert Pegram, which was erected in October 1905. Sir Thomas was a doctor and as an author wrote on subjects such as religion, medicine, science and the esoteric. He was born in October 1605 in Cheapside, London and was educated at Winchester College before graduating from Pembroke College, Oxford. He went on to study medicine abroad, then settled in Norwich and practised medicine up to his death. His first book was *Religio Medici*, which he only showed to friends. An unauthorised edition came out in 1642 and it found its way on to the Papal list of forbidden reading for Catholics. Browne was knighted in 1671 by King Charles II. He died on his 77th birthday and is buried in St. Peter Mancroft Church. In 1840, workmen in the church accidentally opened his coffin. His skull was taken to the Norfolk and Norwich Hospital and was not re-interred until 4th July 1922 where it was registered in the church register as aged 316.

The former Orchard Tavern (seen here in 1937) was originally known as the Orchard Garden and was rebuilt on part of the same site in 1883. When the roads were widened in 1932, the pub again was rebuilt only to be damaged by enemy action on 27th April 1942 and again on 1st May a few days later. Although it looks derelict in the photo, the pub was still trading. In 1945 a wooden hut was built in its place which was still there in 1957 alongside the shell of the original building which was rebuilt again before finally being demolished in 1989.

The site of Murrell's Yard was originally the location of the house belonging to Robert Bell – who was granted the freedom of the city under the reign of King Henry VII. The yard is photographed in dilapidated condition in 1936

The house in the picture dates from the 17th century. All the properties in Murrell's Yard were demolished in 1939 and during the Second World War an air raid shelter took their place.

Heigham Grove House was built in 1803 for Mr Adams, a stonemason from Chapelfield Road. The house had several follies and a three-storey brick clock tower. In 1925 it was purchased by Norwich City Council and then became the city's maternity home. The building was destroyed by a bomb on 27th June 1942.

Eaton Hall on Hurd Road was the house of Alderman Jonathan Davey (1760-1814), a grocer and Baptist radical who built the pedestrian way in what is now known as Davey Place. An alderman is a high-ranking member of a county council and the word is derived from the old English word ealdorman meaning elder man. Eaton Hall became a Grade II listed building on 5th June 1972.

The Austin Friars came to Norwich in the reign of King Edward I and settled in the parish of St. Michael in Conisford. Their founder was Roger Miniot and they were granted a charter in 1293. A hundred years later after acquiring the church of St. Michael and a large part of the parish, they pulled down the church and their old convent and built on the site a cloister and conventional church, meaning that the congregation accepted certain customs and properties. After the Dissolution the friary was granted in the reign of King Edward VI to Sir Thomas Heneage, his wife Catherine and William Lord Willoughby. It later passed on to the Duke of Norfolk who turned it into a garden. The site was later cleared and became a brewery depot. A brewery has been on this site since the 1500s. The Morgan brothers acquired the business in 1844. Watney's took it over in 1963 and in 1971 it was absorbed by Grand Metropolitan who set up the Norwich Brewery. The brewery closed in 1985 and is now a mixture of housing and workshops.

Below: Howard House in King Street took its name from the Duke of Norfolk, who was a Howard in about 1663. It has been suggested that the house was built much earlier as remains were found from the 15th and 16th century which suggests that the house was built over an earlier undercroft. The garden became known as 'My Lord's Garden.' A sundial was on the front of the house dated 1840 with the initials C.S. for Dr. Christopher Spencer who at one stage owned the property. Howard House now forms part of the empty Morgan's brewery building and is in a state of disrepair.

Above: The former Green man pub in King Street opened around 1760 and closed in December 1921 after its licence was refused. It was also known as the Sportsman between 1868 and 1872. After it closed it was converted into houses (as seen here in 1936) but was demolished before the start of the Second World War.

One of the oldest dwellings in Norwich, Music House in King Street was also known as 'Jews House.' Originally built by John Curry, it was sold to Jewish financier Jurnet, and later owned by his son Isaac. There were an estimated 200 Jewish people living in Norwich in the 1100s out of approximately 5,000 of a population. The Jews mainly lived between the castle and the market place for security, as anti-Semitism was rife throughout Europe due to the Crusades. The Jurnet family were very much established when in 1144 a 12 year old skinner apprentice named William was found murdered just outside Norwich. There was no evidence to who had killed him, but the blame soon fell upon the Jews. This became the first so-called 'Blood Libel', which became a widespread belief that the Jews were involved in the ritual murder of Christian children and the drinking of their blood.

Christians were not allowed to lend money which therefore was left to the Jews. By the late 1100s the Jurnet family also had property in London and Kings Lynn. The Jews of England were officially protected by the Crown (to which they lent money) but they were taxed heavily. In 1197 Isaac paid an eighth of the entire tax levied on the city. The Jews of Norwich also helped to gain the release of King Richard I when he was imprisoned in Austria during the Crusade, but Isaac would later suffer the indignity of being arrested and sent to the Tower of London. In 1290 Edward I expelled all the Jews from England.

Lord William de Valeres was given the house by Henry III. In 1613 it was owned by Chief Justice Coke, who had conducted the prosecution for the government of the eight main gunpowder plot conspirators in Westminster Hall in January 1605. During the 19th century, the brewers Youngs, Crawhay and Youngs purchased the house and later presented it to the city. Today it forms part of Wensum Lodge Education Centre.

The Malt House in King Street was owned by Youngs, Crawshay and Youngs. The photo is from 1935,.but the building dates back to the 16th century on the site of the former house of Sir Robert de Salle. In 1381, during the 'Peasants Revolt' for the unpopular poll tax, rebels from Essex and Kent marched to London where they appeared to gain a concession from Richard II until their leader Wat Tyler was murdered. Incidents took place in Norfolk with the burning of the manor court rolls, which recorded tenants' information. Sir Robert made a stand against the men on Mousehold Heath but was murdered.

King Street in 1936 near to Rayners Yard. Near to here was the site of Hildebrond's Hospital. According to the historian Francis Blomefield the hospital was founded in the ancient parish of St. Edward, at the beginning of the 13th century, by Hildebrond le Mercer, citizen, and Maud his wife. It was also known as St. Mary's Hospital, and at a later date was popularly known as Ivy Hall.

Dr. James Flack was one of the founder members of the Medical Institute in Lady's Lane which was founded in 1872 to help the needy with medical expenses. When the National Health Service came in to being, the Medical Institute closed its doors. The Michelin Tyre Company took over the building but it was burnt down on 4th January 1952.

Left: When the city council decided on plans to build a library, Lady's Lane was demolished. Richard Hearne, who was known as TV's Mr. Pastry in the 1940s, 1950s and 1960s was born in Lady's Lane in 1908 and first appeared, aged six months old, with his parents at the Theatre Royal. He went on to be Britain's first television star at the BBC and was their resident clown for 30 years. He also toured America, and appeared on the Ed Sullivan Show many times as well as working with Buster Keaton. A tireless worker for charity, for this he was awarded the O.B.E. In the 1970s he was offered the role of Dr. Who, but wanted to play the role as Mr. Pastry. Producer Barry Letts refused to allow this. Hearne died in 1979.

Right: St. Peter's Wesleyan Church in Lady's Lane was opened in 1824 but was demolished in the 1950s to make way for the central library having been acquired by compulsory purchase by Norwich City Council in 1938. A new church was built by the smaller chapel in Park Lane which opened for worship in 1939 when the Lady's Lane chapel was closed.

Opposite: Frost's and Barrett tool merchants were the principal business in Lobster Lane in 1936. Nearby was the appropiately named Ironmongers Arms. A house was on the site from 1303 and it traded as a pub from 1869 to 2003, the only pub so-named in England. Other businesses included City Wholesale Shoe Co., boot and show factors, Glover and Barnes Ltd., gold blockers, Thorns R. F. & Co, ironmongers, Wilson F. R. & Co., seed growers, and Carruthers Edgar Ltd., drapers.

Miller & Co, cigar merchants and tobacconists were established in 1812. Although photographed in 1934 the Victorian shopfront of 37 London Street was still intact and very much in use. The company boasted that they were the oldest firm of cigar and tobacco dealers in the city. The shop's motto was 'what is pleasure but a pipe?'. A figure of a Highlander stood guard over the shop doorway. By the time the shop eventually closed in the 1970s he had been there for about 150 years. A reporter from the *Evening News* tracked the statue down to America where it was looking very different as it had been repainted.

Thoroughfare Yard runs from 27 Fishergate to 13-15 Magdalen Street. Some of the architecture can be dated back to the late 1600s. The properties were demolished in 1936, the year of this photo, as part of slum clearance. Most of the houses were tiny with families crammed together and sharing outside toilets and wash houses. The families were moved to council estates, including Mile Cross.

The back yard of the White Lion in Magdalen Street. Photographed in 1936 it was demolished later in the 1930s and rebuilt after the Second World War. The White Lion closed in 1962.

Thirtle House in Magdalen Street was named after John Thirtle, the Norwich artist who had a shop here in the early 19th century at No. 26 which provided carving, gilding, frame making and picture restoring. He was also a founder member of the Norwich Society of Artists, but after a row which took place around 1815 he left to join a rival group. After his death, the business was taken over by local artist William Boswell. Thirtle House was demolished in the late 1930s before another building took its place. In that decade there were about 50 food and drinks shops, about 30 pubs, a saddler, a blacksmith and many other trades making Magdalen Street a busy place.

70 Magdalen Street was built in 1813. Stump Cross takes its name from the area which is opposite St. Saviour's Church, the former junction between Magdalen Street and Botolph Street which disappeared when Anglia Square was developed in the late 1960s. The name itself comes from a broken cross that stood there. In the time of Henry VII it was known as Guylding Cross. By 1970 Anglia Square Shopping Centre had been built on the site. At No. 65 was the East Anglian Trustee Savings Bank. Norfolk and Norwich Savings Bank was established by John Hammond Cole, who had previously set up a savings bank in his house in 1812. On the first day of trading, 29th April 1816, 35 accounts were opened. By the 1930s there were branches all over East Anglia and it had been renamed East Anglian TSB.

The White Horse pub's yard in 1936. The pub traded from around 1760 from the site of the former church of St. Buttolph the Abbott which was demolished in the 16th century. The pub closed in May 1955 and was erased in the late 1960s to make way for the Anglia Square shopping development.

These buildings at 92-94 Magdalen Street were said to date from the 17th century and under the 1949 Housing Act they were listed as Grade 3. Hacon's Yard was possibly named after either glove and breeches maker James Hacon, or schoolmaster Charles Hacon. At one stage, the developers for Anglia Square wanted to keep the buildings, but it was not to be and they were demolished.

On 2nd August 1942 incendiary bombs dropped on Hurrell's Shoe Factory at 96-100 Magdalen Street shown here shortly before hostilities commenced. The building was built during the Georgian period and at one stage was the home of John Stainforth Patterson who was sheriff in 1811, alderman in 1820 and mayor in 1823. His father had purchased the property along with Beevor's Brewery, which later became Steward and Patterson. At the end of the Second World War, Hurrell's rebuilt the factory, but it was short-lived as it was demolished to make way for Anglia Square. Hurrell's ceased trading in Norwich in 1962 and its production moved to Portugal. Edward Street now occupies the site.

Gilling's Yard was named after Edmund Gillings, who had a gardening shop in Magdalen Street in the early 1800s. Thomas Arthur Fulcher, a gunner from the 1st East Anglia Brigade who died in action on 4th August 1916, had lived at No. 1 Gilling's Yard with his wife, Rosa May Fulcher.

The White Lion pub at No. 135 traded from 1760 to 1962. The 17th century building was demolished as part of the slum clearance scheme in the 1930s and this yard is now called Hartley's Court.

This sorry-looking building in Mariners Lane was formerly part of the St. John Sepulchre National School. It was erected in 1862, enlarged in 1891 and looked after 310 children, including 134 infants. Miss Lowe was the mistress, whilst Miss Harris was the infants' mistress. On 28th October 1918 the school was temporarily closed because of the influenza epidemic. The school shut for good at the end of July 1930 and the children were placed in other schools in the area.

Georgian shopfront at 1 Market Place photographed in 1935. Thomas Moy Limited, coal and coke manufacturers, were situated all over England. From 1861 the firm was based in Colchester and was described as coal, coke, cement, brick, tile and lime merchants. In the 1880s Moy established a wagon works in Peterborough. The company incorporated in 1891 as Moy's Wagon Co. Ltd. and traded up until the 1960s. Besides distributing solid fuels Thomas Moy Ltd. and various associated companies also sold building supplies and produced agricultural lime.

Below: The listed Guildhall, built between 1407 and 1413, was the seat of local government until 1938 when City Hall was built. Outside of London, it is the largest surviving medieval civic building. Magistrates were still sitting there until 1977 and prisoners were held there up until 1980. A small chapel to cater to their spiritual needs was dedicated to St. Barbara, the patron saint of prisoners. Thomas Bilney was held there on his way to be burnt at the stake at Lollards Pit on 9th August 1531. When the roof collapsed in the late 1500s, Mayor Augustine Steward gathered gifts and donations for its reconstruction in 1534.

The first floor has two main halls which were mainly used for councillors. Around the end of the 17th century Palladian columns were added outside the council chambers. In 1911 the Guildhall had a narrow escape after the city council passed a resolution to have it demolished as it was in disrepair and no longer large enough for their needs, but it was saved after the council decided to go ahead with their plans to build City Hall. The Guildhall was again at risk during the Second World War and in this 1939 photograph it's encircled by a wall of sandbags.

The Guildhall drinking fountain was commissioned and presented in 1859 by philanthropist Charles Pierre Melly. In 1854 John Snow had discovered that cholera was spread by contaminated drinking water and this resulted in widespread commissions for fountains and water pumps, which included the Gurney Obelisk of 1860 on Tombland and those on the Newmarket and Ipswich Roads. Alas it is no longer in working order.

The Villa House in Martineau Lane was situated at Old Lakenham next to the Lakenham swimming pool. The house was built in the middle of the 15th century and had eleven rooms. A wooden panel which had become a cupboard during the 17th century was moved in the 20th century to the Norwich Castle Museum. Two enemy bombs were dropped near to the house in the early hours of 17th May 1941.

This old public house at 80 Oak Street traded between 1806 and closed in 1907. In this 1936 picture it is named The Bess of Bedlam. It had previously been known as Tom of Bedlam and later as The Bedlam and Star of Bethlehem. The area was earmarked early on in the city's slum clearance programme and the site is now occupied by council flats.

This property at Dial Yard was the remains of the house of Gregory Clerk who was sheriff in 1497 and mayor in 1505 and 1514 and so once had been an important and prestigious property. The picture was taken in 1937 just before it was demolished as part of Norwich's slum clearance programme.

In the 19th century Oak Street was filled with narrow buildings, public houses and shops with passageways built through them. Developers purchased plots of land and built on them and the Great Hall lost outbuildings and garden as a result of this, eventually being cut off from Oak Street by the new buildings lining that street. By 1900 there were 750 yards in Norwich housing families in impoverished conditions. A programme of slum clearance programme took place in the 20s and 30s with families being removed to council estates. Many yards survived the slum clearance only to end up being bombed in the Second World War.

From 103 to 119 Oak Street there were up to seven yards, which had been named after public houses or well-known people that lived nearby. In the Key and Castle pub at No. 105 in January 1869 the landlord William Sheward confessed to the police in South London that he had killed his wife Martha eighteen years previously whilst residing at Tabernacle Street. Sheward chopped Martha into small pieces which he stuffed into gullies and drains. It is not known what happened to Martha's head, as William Sheward never told anyone how he had disposed of it. After the guilty verdict was given, Sheward broke down and confessed that a row had taken place at their home and that he cut her throat from ear to ear. He then disposed of the body all over Norwich and told neighbours and friends that she had left him. Sheward married again and his second wife helped to run the Key and Castle. He was hanged by William Calcraft, known for his short drops, in April 1869.

During the 1930s this area had the reputation as being one of the biggest slum areas in Norwich. Nearby to Flower Pot Yard was the Flower Pot public house. It had also been once known as The Flower in Hand and closed in 1907. Enemy action saw Flower Pot Yard almost entirely destroyed, leaving the Great Hall alone in the aftermath after losing most of its outbuildings.

In the 1930s Flower Pot Yard (on the right) was one of the worse slum addresses in Norwich and for this reason in 1931 it was acquired by Major. S. E. Glendenning who wanted to show that the old houses in this area could be rebuilt. Redevelopment work by the Luftwaffe saw most of the surrounding buildings reduced to rubble, as can be seen in this 1955 photo. Major Glendenning owned the Great Hall from 1931 to 1956 and after his death it was sold to Norfolk Archaeological Trust and converted into offices.

Above: The Royal Oak pub at 132 Oak Street dated from the late 16th/early 17th century. The name commemorated the escape of Charles II who hid in the oak tree at Boscabel. The pub was closed in 1940 by its owners Steward and Patterson who notified magistrates that it was to be shut for the duration of the war and it was damaged by enemy action along with other properties on Oak Street on 27th and 29th April 1942. Senior Company Officer NFS Sam Bussey, 39, lost his life whilst on duty fighting the flames. The pub's licence was surrendered in November 1961.

The Tuns Yard behind Oak Street. This had been part of the house of Gregory Clerk, and took its name from the Tuns public house. The area was demolished shortly after this picture was taken in 1937.

In the late 1890s gun maker George Jefferies placed this stag above the shop at 8 Orford Hill. When Darlow's Gun Shop took over they kept it as can be seen from the 1938 photograph. A replica of the stag was put in place in 1984, to speeches made by the Lord Mayor, Stan Peterson, and Mrs V Glauert, head mistress of Blyth-Jex School where the replica was made. Today the Orford Hill dental surgery is located here.

In 1870 the Saddlers Arms merged with the Horse Shoes, which in the 18th century had been known as the Golden Horse Shoes. Called simply the Horse Shoes by the time of this 1939 photograph the pub was damaged by enemy bombs in late April 1942 but survived the war before closing down in February 1959 and the licence transferring to the Heartsease. During the Second World War over 100 pubs in Norwich were lost and in the 1960s many were shut down or demolished. At one stage King Street had 58 pubs and Ber Street had 39.

These houses at nos. 33-35 Pitt Street were demolished in 1937, the year after this photo was taken. A passageway led through them to a chapel at the rear which in 1754 was visited by the brothers and Reverends John and Charles Wesley. In 1818 the stone tablet was placed over the doorway.

Left: Since being divided into two parts of the inner link road, the south part of Pitt Street has become part of Duke Street. The houses shown in this 1936 photograph are from the 18th century and very similar in style. Nos. 60 and 62 fell victim to the bombing raids of 27th and 29th April 1942.

Below:After the demolition of No. 57 Pottergate in January 1983 this 15th century archway was revealed.

Starling Day had his workshop here at 101 Pottergate at the beginning of the 19th century and it was also at one stage the workshop for printers W. J. Pack and Company. Nos. 103 and 105 were badly damaged during bombing in 1942 and were later demolished. Today No. 101 is a residential building.

Starling Day, had been sheriff in 1775 and mayor in 1782 and by 1812 was a wool factor, merchant and banker by trade. He lived here at 103 and 105 Pottergate next to his workshop and opened up a bank in 1795 called Starling Day and Son. The bank later moved to offices near the Market Place and traded until 1825 when it was taken over by Gurney and Co.

The Norvic cinema on Prince of Wales Road opened on Boxing Day 1912 as the Electric and, like many other early cinemas, had live entertainment as well as showing films. It was part of F. H. Cooper's cinema chain. Cooper's head office was situated nearby at Alexandra Mansions. The name changed from Electric to Norvic in 1949 and it became the first cinema in Norwich to be equipped with optical sound films and cinemascope. The Norvic closed in 1959 without any notice and was demolished in 1961. The film showing in this 1961 photo is *The Last Blitzkrieg*, a 1959 Second World War movie produced in Amsterdam by Sam Katzman for Columbia Pictures. Starring Dick York and Kerwin Matthews, the film is a fictional account of Operation Grief in the Battle of the Bulge.

Above: The Great Eastern Hotel at 111 Prince of Wales Road during demolition in 1963. In 1872 the freehold was owned by the Great Hospital Charity and it was known as the Royal Hotel Branch until 1893. It closed in 1961 and after demolition was then rebuilt in 1965 as the Hotel Nelson.

William Vernon Blyth of the Blyth family, who held the licence at one time, was born in Norwich in 1887. He left Norwich Grammar in 1903 to be an engineer with a firm in London, but wanted to become an entertainer and he is better known as dancer Vernon Castle. He and his wife Irene became dancing stars of the day, appearing in Irving Berlin's first Broadway show *Watch Your Step* in 1914. Vernon was a pilot during the First World War, serving with the Royal Flying Corps and was awarded the Croix de Guerre (translating as Cross of War) in 1917. This decoration was created in 1915 and was bestowed on foreign military forces allied to France. He died in a civilian plane crash in February 1918. A film of their life, *The Story of Vernon and Irene Castle* was made by RKO in 1939 starring Fred Astaire and Ginger Rogers.

Right: Robert Garsett, sheriff of Norwich in 1599, lived in Garsett House, also known locally as Armada House. The house has one surviving timber-framed bracket ornately carved with the date 1589, the year of the Spanish Armada. Local tradition states that the timbers used to build the house were salvaged from the ill-fated Spanish Armada, although there had been an earlier house on this site. In 1898 half of the house disappeared to make way for a link road from Redwell Street. Alfred Ernest Kent, a solicitor, lived here and on his death left it to his son Ernest, an antiquarian who in turn bequeathed it to the Norwich and Norfolk Archaeological Society in the early 1900s. The society made the first floor into their library and headquarters. The building is seen here as it was in 1935.

This building at 14 Princes Street was a messuage, a dwelling house of religion with outbuildings and land assigned to it. The street is a piece of picturesque Norwich with its many 16th and 17th century properties and modern offices. Many of the properties were demolished to make way for a shoe factory which itself was then demolished in 1974. No. 14 became a Grade II building in February 1954 and although it was once two houses it is now the offices and home of the Writers Centre.

The former Quayside School photographed in 2000. An artist by trade, Frederick Ellrington Smith was born in Louth, Lincolnshire in 1866. His father was a shipbuilder and he took on his father's skills and many of his own. Educated at a Church of England school in Louth he stayed on as a pupil teacher before studying at Peterborough College. In 1888 he came to Norwich to be a general subjects teacher at Quayside School which was located in the slum area. From here he became head of the art department at the Higher Grade School and also spent twenty years as assistant art master at Norwich Art School, where he had (Sir) Alfred Munnings as his pupil. In 1905 he was given the Royal Humane Society's award for saving a drowning person at Gorleston. He died aged 95 in 1961. Today the building is an apartment block.

This poem was written about the school by one time pupil Bob Littleboy:

They used to say you were half a fool,
If you were sent to Quayside School,
But that's untrue, all the boys I knew
Had all their marbles, and a high I.Q.
Discipline was strict and I'm right to say,
Much more is needed in schools today.
I've seen many a sorry lad limp home,
After a date with "Tubby" in the Science Room.

Not all was dull in our academic lives,
We had football in the playground, or a game of fives.
At sport we had no equals, and at our dinner "Du ",
All the games were resurrected, the goals are scored anew.
Jumbo, Chucky and Ginger Sadd (Frank and Danny too),
Were products of the school, I'm proud to say I knew.
They pursued the noble art, and made their name,
In the toughest sport of all, the boxing game.
It's said a man's character is formed in schoolboy days,
And teachers make an impact in many different ways.
One man we strive to emulate, we will remember him,
With reverence, and kindest thoughts, good old "Pim".
But now we're growing older, and thinner on the ground,
At each Annual Dinner there's less of us around
And while we mourn their passing, one thought cheers,
We're better men for knowing them, over sixty years.
It's nice to know on the other side, lifelong mates,
Will be there to greet you, when you reach the pearly gates
And say "Welcome, Robert, come in and have a jar",
Lead you gently by the hand, to the nearest bar.

At one time called Ferrier House, 3 Queen Street was home to Robertson and Colman, upholsterers and cabinet makers, once known as Robertson and Sons. During the 16th century this building, then a house, was owned by Robert Ferror, who was sheriff in 1507 and mayor in 1526 and again in 1536. In 1922 alterations were made and two important finds were a wooden spandrel carved with a Tudor rose dating from about 1475 and a ceiling composed of moulded beams which formed a number of rectangles. Opposite here is St. Mary the Less which from 1959 to 1985 was used as a warehouse for the company. The building until recently housed a branch of the ill-fated Bank of Scotland but is currently vacant and empty.

Old Bank of England Court, Queen Street photographed in 1936. A branch of said bank traded here from 1828 to 1852, one of a number of occupants of note in the years before and after. In 1798 Fosters the solicitors were here. William Foster III was an expert carriage driver who won a bet that he could turn round a coach and horses in the small courtyard. The Norfolk and Norwich Art Circle (1885-1985) held their classes here. Architect Edward Boardman (1833-1910) also had his office here and one of the spandrels has his initials 'EB' intertwined and the other has the date '1875'. The entrance is still decorated with a mosaic floor. There is also a personalised terracotta name plate and a monogrammed ceramic decoration, much of which came from the Gunton Works at Costessey and is known as Costessey-ware. The firm of Edward Boardman and Sons was established in 1860 by Mr. Alderman Edward Boardman. His son, Edward T. Boardman, joined in 1889. One of the most important public buildings designed by Boardman was the Norfolk and Norwich Hospital when it was rebuilt on the old site in 1882. Other buildings designed by Boardman were the electricity works in Duke Street, the Jenny Lind Infirmary, A. J. Caley & Sons, Laurance, Scott & Co's warehouse at Carrow Works, Haldinstein's Shoe Factory in Queen Street, the Norfolk News Company in London Street, Harmer's Works, and Howlett & White Limited.

A 1962 picture of Queens Road Tower. In October 1908 Norwich Council requested a report on the city wall. Two tears later the city engineer, Arthur Collins, presented his report, but in 1914 works were suspended because of the outbreak of war. The widening of St. Stephen's Street in the early 1960s provided the opportunity to open up a length of wall along Chapelfield Road and Queens Road. The tower, which was at the back of 8 Queens Road was described as "A bit of old rubbish" by one councillor. After many meetings, the adjoining wall went and the tower was allowed to stay. Alas, by 1964 the two 14th century gun posts had been vandalised. Queens Road was the birthplace of Geoffrey Watling in April 1913. During the course of his life Geoffrey had over 200 different businesses. After the Second World War he owned several cafés and opened the Rainbow Ice Cream factory at Great Yarmouth and also bought the Samson and Hercules ballroom on Tombland. He loved big band music and had soon also purchased the Kessingland Palais Ballroom at Lowestoft and the Lido Ballroom on Aylsham Road. He also had an interest in the Hammersmith Palais Ballroom in London. After selling the Samson and Hercules to Mecca he purchased Jarretts Removals, Shipdham Car Hire Services, Beeline Taxis and the transport side of Fitt Funeral Services. He soon had an interest in Crown Cruises in Norwich, the local Bell Fruit gambling machine franchise. By the time he was 70 and semi-retired he still had up to twenty businesses left. He had a love of fast cars and had the number plates GW80 and GW444. He also owned three boats and raced at Oulton Broad in the 1950s. It is considered that he helped to save Norwich City Football Club in 1956 and became one of its longest-serving chairmen.

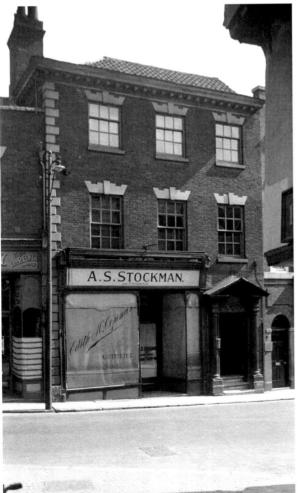

Above: The three storey house in this 1936 picture of Nos. 11-13 Rampant Horse Street was known as Mingay House. The corner itself was known as St. Stephen's Church Lane. C. S. Rosson & Co traded here as gun manufacturers. Charles Stanley Rosson was the son of the Derby gun maker Charles Rosson, who acquired 13 Rampant Horse Street, which had been occupied by different gun makers for decades. The firm had started trading in 1825. Charles continued running the business in Derby whilst Charles Stanley ran the Norwich business. Charles died in 1912 and Charles Stanley became the sole owner of the business, which also housed offices, a cartridge loading room, workshops and stores. Many of the landed gentry were customers. In the 1930s a gun showroom was built with a glass roof to ensure the maximum light for clients to view the guns. During the Luftwaffe Baedeker raids of April 1942, the premises were totally destroyed. For the rest of the war the company traded in a limited way from the premises of Gallyon & Sons in Kings Lynn. By 1945 they were trading in White Lion Street before moving to 7 Bedford Street. They were bought out by Gallyon & Sons Ltd. in May 1965.

Left: This picture from 1939 shows the firm of A. S. Stockman, ladies outfitters, formerly known as Edith M. Copeman, who had premises in 14 Rampant Horse Street. Until December 1933 the firm had been a partnership between Copeman and Annie Stanley Stockman. A previous occupier was John Mackerell, whose son Benjamin produced historical manuscripts of Norwich and the parishes of St. Peter Mancroft and St. Stephen's.

Opposite: Clement Court is situated at 2-3 Redwell Street and is where Frances Burges published the first edition of the *Norwich Post* in 1701. In the middle 1700s Francis Christien and his son Edward ran a dancing ballroom and academy here. By the early 20th century it was a chapel then later to 1947 was the laboratory of the city analyst. When Norfolk News Company extended their London Street offices in 1957 and moved here the houses in Clement Court were demolished.

Foundry Bridge is a wrought iron, single span bridge and is the third to have been built on the site since 1810-11. The first bridge provided access to the iron foundry and stood on the River Wensum. This was replaced in 1844 when the train station was built on the old foundry site. The area by the station soon became crowded with houses and hotels for the railway workers and as factories were built by the river the station was rebuilt in 1866. The Great Eastern Hotel which stood beside the bridge was demolished in 1963. In this photograph from 1934 the *Rotterdam* is moored near the bridge.

Pykerell's house in Rosemary Lane was a 15th century merchant's house, first known as Pilgrim's Hall and built by Thomas Pykerell who was mayor in 1525, 1533 and 1538. From the 19th century until 1908 it was the Rosemary Tavern. In 1902 landlord William Spatchett, like so many other Norwich licensees, was convicted of opening out of hours and was fined. The house was saved for clearance by being purchased by the Norfolk Archaeological Trust and is seen here in 1935. During the bombings of 1942 the thatch was burnt off and much damage was done to the building, but it was saved by the Ancient Monuments Division of the Ministry of Works, who stopped the proposed demolition.

This small triangular-shaped house was where the artist, Robert Ladbrooke, died in October 1842. Scoles Green was originally known as Scholars Green as a school was located here before the Reformation and it was near to the church of St. Martin in Balliva. It is now the offices of Archant who publish the *Norwich Evening News*, the *EDP* and many other regional newspaper titles.

This building in Silver Street dates from 1907 and was the depot for the tram network for Norwich from 1901 to 1935. The very last service to operate was between Newmarket Road and Cavalry Barracks via Riverside Road, with the final car leaving Orford Place at 11:10pm on 10th December 1935 to the accompaniment of the crowd singing *Auld Lang Syne*. When the car arrived at the depot *Auld Lang Syne* was sung again. By 1955, when the photograph was taken, this was the only place where the track remained, but at its height there had been 50 trams, each with 52 seats, and seven routes. The company shown is Kearley & Tonge Ltd, which later became part of International Stores which developed into the first modern supermarket chain.

The Prince of Denmark pub started out as a free house in 1839 and over the years was owned by Morgans, Allsopp & Co, Bullards, Watney Mann, Courage, Spring Inns and Inntrepreneur. Landlord Thomas Rix was convicted in 1916 of 'failing to close against' soldiers i.e. serving them with drink and was fined ten shillings or seven days detention. After the start of the First World War The Defence of the Realm Act was passed by Parliament. This restricted the opening times of licensed premises.

Named after the Suckling family who owned the property in the 16th century part of Suckling House can be traced back to the 13th century when William de Rollesby lived there in 1285. Many bailiffs, merchants, sheriffs and mayors subsequently purchased the property. Robert Suckling, sheriff in 1564 and mayor in 1572 and 1582, bought it in the middle 1500s. His son, Edmund, became dean of Norwich in 1614 and another son, Sir John, inherited the house in 1589 and sold it in 1595. Sir John went on to become secretary of state to James I and Charles I. Lord Horatio Nelson's great aunt was a Suckling and lived here also. The house was last used as a residence in 1915. It was occupied by The Norfolk News Company Ltd. in 1916 and in 1923 was purchased by Ethel Mary and Helen Caroline Colman. The Duke of York opened it to the public on October 25th 1925 and is still open today as Cinema City and a restaurant.

The doorway to the Bridewell on St. Andrews Hill dates from 1490 and was originally one of three entrances to the building. Doubts have been cast as to whether it is in its original location as the brick wall around the door dates from the late 18th century.

The city library, the first in England, was set up in May 1608 and had three rooms. It remained as a reference library until 1716 when it was agreed that books could be borrowed. The new free library which opened in March 1857 is shown here in 1955 but was demolished when the new central library was opened in January 1963.

In 1654 Thomas Symonds was the first Quaker in Norwich. Around 1670 the Norwich Quakers purchased an acre of land from St. Augustine's Parish from the Great Hospital. Land was also purchased in 1694 to build a meeting house at Gildencroft (seen here in 1934) and in 1699 the first meeting was held there. The Quakers also built houses which were rented out to their fellow Quakers. The cottages have survived and are said to be the largest continuous row of Tudor cottages still standing in England. In 1813 the Jewish community leased land in the Gildencroft to use as a cemetery and in 1892 Norwich City Corporation bought the Gildencroft and it became a public park.

Cardinal Cap's Yard took its name from the adjacent public house and is believed to date back to 1760. It's seen here in 1936 and although war-damaged in 1942 the building survived until 1963. The origin of the pub's name probably comes from when Cardinal Wolsey visited Norwich in 1517 and 1520.

Greyfriars, dedicated to St. Francis, was founded in 1226 and was built on the site which is now Prince of Wales Road. In 1539 the property was given to Thomas, Duke of Norfolk, Earl Marshall of England, but was seized by the king in 1544 and given to Paul Gresham and Francis Bolders. In 1559 it was sold to the city and most of the buildings were dismantled. Extensive archaeological excavations were carried out between 1992 and 1995 when the site was developed for residential use.

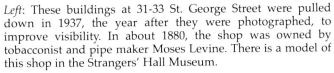

Left: These buildings at 31-33 St. George Street were pulled down in 1937, the year after they were photographed, to improve visibility. In about 1880, the shop was owned by tobacconist and pipe maker Moses Levine. There is a model of this shop in the Strangers' Hall Museum.

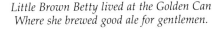

Right: Until the air raid of 1942, the Golden Can was situated at 90 St. George Street. The golden can was a variation of the beer vessel theme seen on many pub signs, harking back to the times when many potential customers could not read and a pictorial sign had to say it all. An old nursery rhyme went:

Little Brown Betty lived at the Golden Can
Where she brewed good ale for gentlemen.

1932

1934

The Norwich Hippodrome, designed by W. G. R. Sprague, was built on the site of the Norfolk Hotel and was known as the Grand Opera House as at the time there was already a Hippodrome in Theatre Street. The first play to be performed (in August 1903) was *The Country Girl*. In 1904 the Grand Opera House and the Hippodrome decided to swap names. Although it was granted a cinematography licence in 1911, it didn't operate as a full-time cinema until September 1931 when the first talkie to be screened was *Condemned* starring Ronald Colman. Great names who appeared here Charlie Chaplin, Laurel and Hardy, Marie Lloyd, Gracie Fields and Archibald Leak (Cary Grant). ABC Cinemas had the contract to show films until 1937, at which time it reverted to being a theatre. During the bombings of April 1942, the Hippodrome was hit, killing the manager. Variety came back to the Hippodrome in the 1950s and to keep the venue open striptease artists appeared, but despite this the building was demolished in 1964 and a car park took its place.

1960

12 St. Giles Street was a Georgian mansion seen on entering Low's Yard. Shown as it was in 1934, the house was demolished in 1938 when City Hall was built on the site. The yard was named after veterinary surgeon Frederick Low who lived in this house for many years. The doorway was saved and placed in the Bridewell Museum.

Sir Thomas Churchman (1702-1791) alderman of St. Stephen's Ward in 1759 and mayor in 1761 built the property known as Churchman House at what is now 71 Bethel Street (formerly 68 St. Giles' Street). His memorial can be found in St. Giles Church. In February 1875 the house became Norwich High School for Girls. The property later was in the ownership of Sir Peter Eade, consultant physician at the Norfolk and Norwich Hospital. Sir Peter was sheriff in 1880-1 and mayor in 1883, 1893 and 1895. He died in 1915 aged 90. Today Churchman House is the Norfolk Register Office.

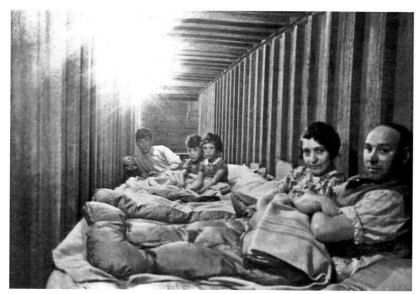

This picture shows the caretaker of Churchman House, Charles Harmer and his family in the air raid shelter at 68 St. Giles Street during bombing raids in 1940.

Right: To the left of this 1936 picture of St. Gregory's Alley are flyers for cinema and theatre attractions. Showing at the Carlton Super Cinema is *Whipsaw* starring Spencer Tracy and Myrna Loy, in which a government agent pretends to be a crook and travels across the country with a lady thief. Also showing is *Fighting Youth* with Charles Farrell and June Martel, in which communist subversives try to take over a college. At the Haymarket is *The Widow from Monte Carlo*, an American comedy featuring Warren William, Dolores del Rio and Louise Fazenda, and *Shadows of the Orient*, a B feature about human smuggling.

Left: This row of houses at 4-5 St. George's Alley were situated near to the Maddermarket Theatre. A passageway by two of the houses led to Farnell's Court named after Farnell, a fine pensman who compiled copy books that were used in most of the schools in Norwich in around the 1830s.

The Palace Works were originally established for the production of oil and gas for the then existing factories in the city. In 1824 the British Gaslight Company bought the works. The old retort house, which had a one million cubic feet capacity, was taken down and replaced with a 2.5 million cubic feet retort house fully equipped with coal and coke handling plant. The retort house was 200 feet long, 70 feet wide and 50 feet to the wall plates. The gas works closed down in the early 1960s and on the site now is part of the Norwich Magistrates, Crown and County courts.

Farnell's Court was demolished in 1953 during the extension to the Maddermarket Theatre.

Where the magistrates' court now stands used to be Beehive Yard and the Beehive public house at 17-18 St. Martin's Palace Plain. The houses were three storey Georgian mansions.

This site at 17 St. Martin's Palace Plain is now occupied by the Magistrates' Court. An excavation in 1981 revealed late Saxon period buildings, most likely which were warehouses. Saxon burials were also found, as were metal objects and pottery sherds from the middle Saxon to post-medieval periods.

The Cupid Bow public house at 23 St. Martin-at-Palace Plain closed in 1917. The lease had expired and not been renewed and the licence was finally lost in 1919. The owners, Youngs and Co., did this as it allowed them to close it without the complication of a compensation hearing. The photograph shows it in 1938, but it was not demolished until 1968.

The White Swan Inn at 31 St. Peter's Street was sometimes known as the Swan Inn or the Swan Hotel and dated back to 1648. Seen here at the end of its days in 1961 it was demolished later that decade to make way for a car park.

Thomas Osborn Springfield lived here at 5 St. Mary's Alley and this 1938 photo shows the splendid Georgian doorway. He was sheriff in 1827 and mayor in 1829 and 1836. Born in 1782 he started as a watch and clock maker in Colegate and went on to become head of a large firm of silk makers. He died in April 1858 and is buried in the Rosary Cemetery.

Below: This 1935 photograph shows the entrance in St. Peter's Street to Mancroft Yard. The Free Trade Tavern or Inn was damaged by bombs on two separate occasions in late April 1942. It stood on the south west corner of St. Peter Mancroft Church and was demolished in the 1960s to make way for the central library and the associated car park.

Opposite: At 7 St. Peter's Street was the Beehive pub which closed in 1927 seven years before this photograph. In 1868 it was known as the Beehive Wine and Spirit Vaults, then from the early 1870s to the 1920s it was Anthony's Wine and Spirit Vaults. The pub was demolished in the 1930s to make way for City Hall.

Opposite: This photo from 1940 shows a 17th century ceiling panel at 12 St. Stephen's Street. Barwell's the wine merchants traded from here before it was lost to wartime bombings. Earlier owners of the building included Thomas de Bokenham, who was mayor in 1479 and 1486, and Robert de Burgh, who was sheriff in 1494 and mayor in 1504. Thomas Petingale took over the property in 1547 and he later sold it to Alderman Nicholas Baker, who had it from 1576 to 1626. A stone built into the property had the initials W./J.s F. and the date 1668. Later owners included Francis Tavernier, 'Oylman' of London, Alderman Goodman and Parrott Hanger, and Colonel Knipe Gobbett. There were eight rectangular panels. Four displayed large cornucopias figured in high relief, two had a female figure, one held an anchor symbolising hope and the other carried a book and a lamp. The remaining two panels were blank.

Above: The houses at 24 St. Saviour's Lane, shown here as they were in 1936, have all now gone but had dated from the 16th to the 19th century. High-Tech House was built in 1938 and was occupied by Mansfield's cardboard box factory who moved along from No. 24, a Georgian mansion called Pendleton House, the house in the centre of the photograph. Mrs. Elizabeth Pendleton, who owned property in the lane and at St. Stephen's in the 17th century, was the original owner. Her will stated that her properties should be used for charitable purposes. Rents from her houses went towards clothing the poor and the needy, and to give loans to young tradesmen.

In 1915 the Great Eastern Railway Company offered the city council £10,000 towards the project of widening St. Stephen's Street as they wanted a grander and more spacious approach to the station. The offer was refused and as a result Victoria Station (on the site of the present-day Sainsbury's) was closed and passengers were diverted to Norwich Station (at that time Thorpe Station). The road-widening issue was looked at again in the 1930s. Nearby stood the Boar's Head Inn and the Crown and Angel public house. During the air raids of 1942 the Boar's Head, along with Barwell's wine and spirit merchants and several factory buildings of Caley's, were destroyed. In 1953 demolition began as part of the road-widening but was not completed until the early 1960s.

Built in the 1960s, 40 to 46 St. Stephen's Street was originally a branch of Woolworths and Sainsbury's. It is now the entrance to Chapel Field shopping mall.

The Crown and Angel public house at 41 St. Stephen's Street was destroyed by bombing along with Crown and Angel Yard in 1942. It is now the entrance to Chapel Field shopping mall.

Caley's chocolate factory chimney before the widening of St. Stephen's Street. It was later demolished to make way for Chapel Field shopping centre.

Barwell's Court off St. Stephen's Street in 1955 with Marks and Spencer on the far left. The store first opened at 17 St. Stephen's Street in 1912 and closed in 1926. Throughout the 1930s and 1940s Marks and Spencer did not trade in Norwich, but as part of a post-war expansion a new store opened between Rampant Horse Street and St. Stephen's Street in March 1950, and in 1955 it extended into Barwell's Court. The building has undergone many changes, but remained the Norwich home of Marks n Sparks ever since. On the right is H. Samuel, which started in 1862 when Harriet Samuel from Great Yarmouth took over the clock-making business of her father-in-law in Liverpool. The business moved to Manchester and subsequently Harriet's son developed it as a retailer.

This thatched house in St. Swithin's Alley was refurbished in the 1930s by the Norwich Amenities Preservation Society. Other properties nearby which were built in the 17th century became the St. Swithin's parsonage then later became tenements but were pulled down in 1938. The Hampshire Hog was at the rear but its licence was given up in 1912. Landlord John Pratt was convicted in 1885 for allowing consumption out of hours and was fined £2 plus 8/- costs. Under his boxing name of John 'Licker' Pratt, he won the first public boxing match in Norwich with Jem Mace who went on to become the first heavyweight champion of the world. Mace had been the landlord of The White Swan in Swan Lane in 1858-59.

Before the Second World War this four-storey building at 1 Surrey Street was owned by Gerald Spalding who used it as a stationer's shop and post office. The building was boarded up in 1942 and escaped the serious damage that was suffered by its neighbours. It was removed in 1962 as part of the road-widening scheme of St. Stephen's Street.

14-21 Ebenezer Terrace. The terrace was situated behind 35 Sussex Road. Mr. Wright, who lived in Spencer Road, was the rent collector for the tenants of Ebenezer Terrace and would also turn up in a pony and trap from which he sold small bags of coal, chopped wood, vegetables, apples and pears. If you took a carrot for the pony you might be lucky and get a hard-boiled sweet.

This photo shows nos. 15-25 Synagogue Street in 1938. The synagogue was built in 1848 and destroyed during enemy action in 1942. It was the only street so-named in the UK. In 1847 Thomas Smithdale established the St. Anne's Foundry at St. Anne's Wharf on the corner of this street. St. Faiths Tavern stood on the corner with Mountergate Street. White's Directory of 1883 showed the following residing on street: Jews' Synagogue. Rev. Heim Newmann (rabbi), Mrs. Susanna Hicklenton, Mrs. Elizabeth S. Sexton, William Allthorpe (foreman), Robert P. Woods, (confectioner's assistant), William England (coal merchant), John England (coal merchant), Richard Worsley (maltster), T. & Son Smithdale (engineers), and William Rudd (wood turner).

Trowse Yard was located between 10 and 14 Ten Bell Lane and was possibly named after the tailor Christopher Trowse who worked there. These houses were demolished in 1938 as part of the slum clearance programme and the yard was demolished soon afterwards.

The Shakespeare public house shown here in 1938 closed in 1964 and was then demolished. In the centre of the front elevation was a sculpted portrait of William Shakespeare.

In 1951, the council put up stalls on brick and concrete foundations in Tombland, but the Norwich Society objected sufficiently to go to court and gain an injunction. The stalls were replaced by mobile vans.

14 Tombland was built around 1504 and in 1530 was rebuilt by Augustine Steward. Born in 1491, Steward was mayor three times in the 16th century. In 1549 the house was used as the headquarters of the two royal armies sent to fight Kett's Rebellion. The house was restored in 1900 and again in 1944 when the roof was damaged by fire. It still stands today and is an antiques centre.

Government agency the Milk Marketing Board was established in 1933 to control distribution and production and had its Norwich base at 4-14 Unthank Road. The road is named after the Unthank family. William Unthank became a freeman of Norwich in 1752 and was in business in St. Stephen's as a corn merchant, barber, peruke (wig) maker, salesman and coach letter. In 1949 the year of this photograph Mr. and Mrs. Oakley lived above the premises having moved there from a terraced home in Theatre Street. The building still stands and is a mixture of commercial and residential use.

During the redevelopment of the link road, the six former almshouses at 68-78 West Pottergate, photographed in 1962, were demolished. Pye's almshouses were originally built near St. Gregory's Church and in 1614 were given by Thomas Pye to the poor over the age of 50. In 1827 the houses were given by the corporation to Joseph Bexfield in exchange for these newly-built cottages and £200 towards the upkeep. The six people chosen to live here came from the parishes of St. Michael Coslany, St. Giles and St. Peter Mancroft.

The Yarn Factory was built in 1836. Until the Reformation this land was part of Cowgate, which was occupied by the monastery of the Carmelites, or Whitefriars who had been there since 1256. In 1904 the foundations were uncovered and in 1920 some pieces of window tracery were found and built into a wall at Factory Yard. They were removed when Jarrolds built onto their works. The 14th century archway is now housed at the Magistrates' Court.

Formerly called Church Street (and now William Booth Street) this was the home of Walter Haydon, bookbinder, Sadd & Linay, solicitors and Joshua Smith, shoe clicker. In the 1950s this was a thriving commercial area, with a cafe and a poodle parlour on the east side and on the west side a flower seller and the George and Dragon pub.

In 1913 Borrow House (in Borrow's Court in Willow Lane) was opened as a museum by Arthur Michael Samuel who went on to become the first Jewish lord mayor. Author George Borrow was born in East Dereham in July 1803 to Thomas, an army recruiting officer and Anne, and lived in this house during his youth with his father. Educated at Norwich Grammar School, it was thought that he would have a career in law, but he became interested in literature. From 1825 he visited many countries as an agent for the Bible Society, learning about people and their languages. His literary works, written after his marriage of 1840 when he settled in Lowestoft, were a mixture of fiction travel writing and linguistics and used his experiences abroad as source material. His best-known works are *The Zincali* (1841), *The Bible in Spain* (1843), *Lavengro* (1851), *The Romany Rye* (1852), *Wild Wales* (1862) and *Romano Lavo-Lil* (1874).

This pair of thatched cottages in Windmill Alley, Ber Street photographed in 1935 were burnt down at the same time as Bonds and St. Michael-at-Thorn. The cottages had only had their roofs repaired five years earlier.

Every city and town in the country decorated their streets and premises to celebrate the 1935 Royal Silver Jubilee to mark 25 years of George V being on the throne. Norwich City Council organised a street procession for the afternoon of Jubilee Day, May 6th, and appealed to the citizens of Norwich to decorate their premises for a week. The committee also decided to award three Silver Jubilee cups as prizes for the best-decorated business premises, and the same number for the best-decorated private houses, as well as a certificate awarded to the trading organisation whose area contained the best decorated street.

The Norwich Chamber of Commerce, at the request of the city council, agreed to be responsible for the organisation of the procession. Apart from decorated vehicles (note "Hitler" saluting to the adoring crowds), tableaux, and walkers in fancy dress, a special section was included for the many organisations such as Boy Scouts, Girl Guides, C.E.Y.M.S., Y.M.C.A., Salvation Army, etc., to be represented. The procession assembled in Newmarket Road before setting off.

Below: The Royal Hotel had previously been on Gentleman's Walk, now home to the Royal Arcade. The site for the new hotel in Agricultural Plain was originally owned by the firm of solicitors Fosters, Burroughs and Robberds. Designed by the Norwich architect Edward Boardman, it was built by John Young and Son. Guntons of Costessey supplied the decorative brickworks, known as Costessey-ware. Permission was required and given by Queen Victoria to name the hotel 'Royal.' The Royal Hotel had its grand opening on 16th November 1897 with a luncheon for over 100 people. Sir. Harry Bullard MP from the Bullard Brewery Company made a toast to the 'very elegant palace that has been erected'.

Orford Place decorated for the Silver Jubilee. A horse-drawn bus service was in operation by the Norwich Omnibus Company from 1879, and in 1897, after an act of parliament, Norwich City Council approved the construction of an electric tram service that would be run by the Norwich Electric Tramways Company. It took two years to complete and the power plants were supplied by the Westinghouse company. Large crowds waited on the streets on 30th July 1900 to watch the first trams in operation. By 1904 the Orford Place track was made more accessible and in 1928 a passenger shelter was put in place by Walter MacFarlane and Co., of Glasgow. The wages for a conductor were 3d. per hour and the motor men were paid 4d. per hour. A story states that in the early days of the trams, Alderman Green, who had a gent's outfitters and drapery in the Haymarket got on a tram and was approached by Inspector Hunt who asked to see his ticket. Alderman Green stated that he had dropped his ticket whilst giving up his seat to a lady. Inspector Hunt demanded that he find the ticket, but Alderman Green stated that he was not going to crawl on the floor to look for a ticket and that his word should be taken as a gentleman. The inspector refused and pressed charges against Alderman Green who was fined five pounds. Legend states that after this incident, Alderman Green purchased a cane and struck a tram stand every time he passed one. There were seven routes in Norwich. The white route was Unthank Road and Denmark Street. The red route was Earlham Road and Thorpe Road, the green route was Newmarket Road and Cavalry Road , which in the summer months was extended to Mousehold Heath, the orange route was Orford Place to Trowse, the yellow and red route was Orford Place to City Road, the red and blue route was Aylsham Road to the Royal Hotel and the blue route was positioned at the Royal Hotel and went to the top of the hill on Dereham Road by Merton Road. Further routes were run along Chapel Field Road and Theatre Street via Rampant Horse Street for a bypass when Orford Place was locked during busy times of the day. In March 1930, the Orford Place and Trowse Station route was closed down and in December 1933 the Eastern Counties Omnibus Company purchased a controlling interest in The Norwich Electric Tramcar Company and replaced the trams with buses.

Chamberlin's store was located on Guildhall Hill and from the late 19th century onwards people came from all over East Anglia to shop there. Henry Chamberlin came to Norwich from Edinburgh in 1814 and set up the department store. In 1823 his son Robert joined him as a partner and the firm became known as Chamberlin Sons & Company. Robert took the company to new heights. By 1848 he had entered politics to become sheriff. He was alderman in 1870 and mayor three times. Married twice, he had seventeen children; two of them, Alexander and George joined the firm and played a pivotal role in the store's development. The company had a factory in Botolph Street and during the First World War it was employed solely to produce civilian goods for home and abroad and became the sole concessionaires in the manufacture of Pegamoid waterproof clothing. It was also involved with the manufacture of East Coast Oilskin waterproof materials. Many of the staff enlisted to serve in the war and casualties amounted to eight. When you visited the store you would be greeted by a floor walker, served by a member of staff who had been there for some years standing, as those working between one and two years would fetch and carry for their superiors.It would only be after serving three years that they would be able to deal with customers directly.

Palmer's in Red Lion Street started life in Great Yarmouth in 1837 when Garwood Burton Palmer opened what was a small drapery store. Garwood's brother Nathanial Benjamin came to the business in 1844 and was soon made a full partner. He died at the relatively young age of 38 and his sons, Edward Earnest and James Hurry joined the business in 1874 and 1876 respectively. Garwood died in 1888, leaving his two nephews in charge. By 1908, Garwood's great nephew Percy Hurry was owner. Percy's son-in-law Graham Sturrock joined the firm in 1947 and became chairman in 1960. His son Bruce joined in 1971, becoming managing director in 1983 and chairman in 1993. His sister, Wendy Cole, who had been a fashion buyer at Bloomingdales in New York, joined as fashion director in 1993. They represent the fifth generation of family management.

The Jarrolds came to England in 1688 with King William of Orange. John Jarrold started the business in 1770, aged 25 in Woodbridge, Suffolk and died five years later. The business was carried on by trustees until 1785 when John Jarrold II took over and a printing press was established. In 1823 John moved to Norwich and set up business in London Street with his son John James, and was soon joined by another son, Samuel. In 1831 son William Pightling joined, followed in 1832 by Thomas. In 1850, John James started a school for children in two cottages situated in Silver Road. Thomas was a member of the corporation as a tax commissioner and was also a member of the board of the Norfolk and Norwich Hospital. In 1881, William T. F. Jarrold joined the business and in 1892 he entered the corporation as a representative for Earlham Ward. The picture shows Jarrolds shop decorated for the 1937 Coronation of King George VI and Queen Elizabeth.

Wincarnis was originally made from port wine and Liebig's extract of meat and malt. It was advertised as being the finest tonic and restorative and was produced from 1881 by Coleman and Co. Ltd in Westwick Street. It was later part of Bass before being sold in 1998 to Ian MacLeod Distillers of Broxburn for whom it is produced by Broadland Wineries in Norfolk.

Below: Orford Place won second prize for the 1937 Coronation street decoration party.

Ruth E. Hardy was a leading figure in the local Independent Labour Party and the first female socialist and married woman to be lord mayor (1950-1951). She invited Princess Elizabeth to come to Norwich to open the Norwich Festival which was opened with a special civic service in Norwich Cathedral on Sunday 17th June followed by a decorated procession.